ELEPHANTS
GENTLE GIANTS OF KAPAMA

van den berg

ELEPHANTS
GENTLE GIANTS OF KAPAMA

photographed by
HEINRICH VAN DEN BERG
PHILIP & INGRID VAN DEN BERG
at Kapama Private Game Reserve

published by
HPH PUBLISHING

There is a mystery behind that grey visage, an ancient life force, delicate and mighty, awesome and enchanted, commanding the silence ordinarily reserved for mountain peaks, great fires and the sea.

Peter Matthiessen, *The Tree Where Man Was Born*

Elephants never pass unnoticed. Their mere presence commands respect and their enormous size instils quiet awe. Yet there's a kindred spirit between the giant pachyderms and frail humans that is clearly evident on eye contact. Compassion and tenderness towards their young and extended family members give elephants a certain human quality. They never forget and pass down knowledge to their offspring regarding survival strategies, social graces, best behaviours and migratory paths tramped by their ancestors to secure food and water. Elephants appear to mourn their dead and have been seen lifting and stroking the bones of dead family members, as if performing a ritual of respect. These animals appear to have a wisdom that transcends their animal kingdom. It's as if they know much more than they're telling.

Yet elephants are not all grace and charm. When threatened, these docile animals can become giant packages of fury, trumpeting in shrill tones to evoke terror and flapping their enormous ears to appear even more ominous. As conservationist Joyce Poole aptly says: "Whether sad or angry, distressed, eager or playful, elephants are this in a big way,"

There's ongoing debate regarding the intelligence of elephants. They have the largest brain of all land mammals and similar cerebral development to that in humans. Yet, proportionately, the brain of an elephant is still smaller than that of a human being. Still, it's curious that an elephant's brain grows by 65% during its lifetime, and the brain of man by 75%. Other mammals – excluding the great apes – only develop their brains by about 10% during their life span.

This highly-evolved brain function may be the key to the superior memory and intelligence of elephants – and their numerous unmistakeable similarities to human beings. Even ancient Greek philosopher Aristotle remarked that the elephant "passeth all others in wit and mind". But can humans really be that similar to a wild animal?

There is a well-recognised link between intelligence and complex social structure. Humans have this attribute and possibly so do elephants. In elephant society the family group is the core social unit, which is headed by a matriarch accompanied by female relatives and their offspring. Male elephants leave this core group when they reach puberty. High-ranking bulls and those in musth do keep regular contact with the breeding herds for both social reasons and mating.

Here they share another similarity with humans, being the only other mammal where the life span of females extends beyond the age of reproduction. Elephants can easily live as long as 70 years. The oldest cow is deemed to have the greatest wisdom and life experience and is often the leader of the herd. The death of such an elephant usually has a devastating effect on the herd, which appears to grieve and mill around the body for days as if holding a wake for the dead leader.

It is such displays of tenderness that make elephants so endearing, along with the patience and guidance shown toward their young. It is almost paradoxical to see elephants display such gentleness when they are of the largest and most powerful animals on earth. With extreme tolerance they discipline their young, put up with their tantrums when they are weaned and lead by example. In between, there is always time for affection and play. Even after independence, young elephants always maintain close relationships with their families and show great excitement when meeting each other.

Without being anthropomorphic, we do seem to recognise distinct similarities between ourselves and elephants: the importance of family, respect for elders, memory of the past. At the very least there is great affinity and mutual respect between elephant and man. At most, elephants are more like us than we care to admit.

THE ELEPHANT OF AFRICA

The scientific name of the African elephant is <u>Loxodonta africana africana</u>. The largest land mammal is easily recognised by its two tusks extending from the upper jaw, its trunk and very large ears. Males can reach a shoulder height of up to four metres and a mass of 5000 to 6000kg. Females are smaller and are approximately two thirds of the male's weight.

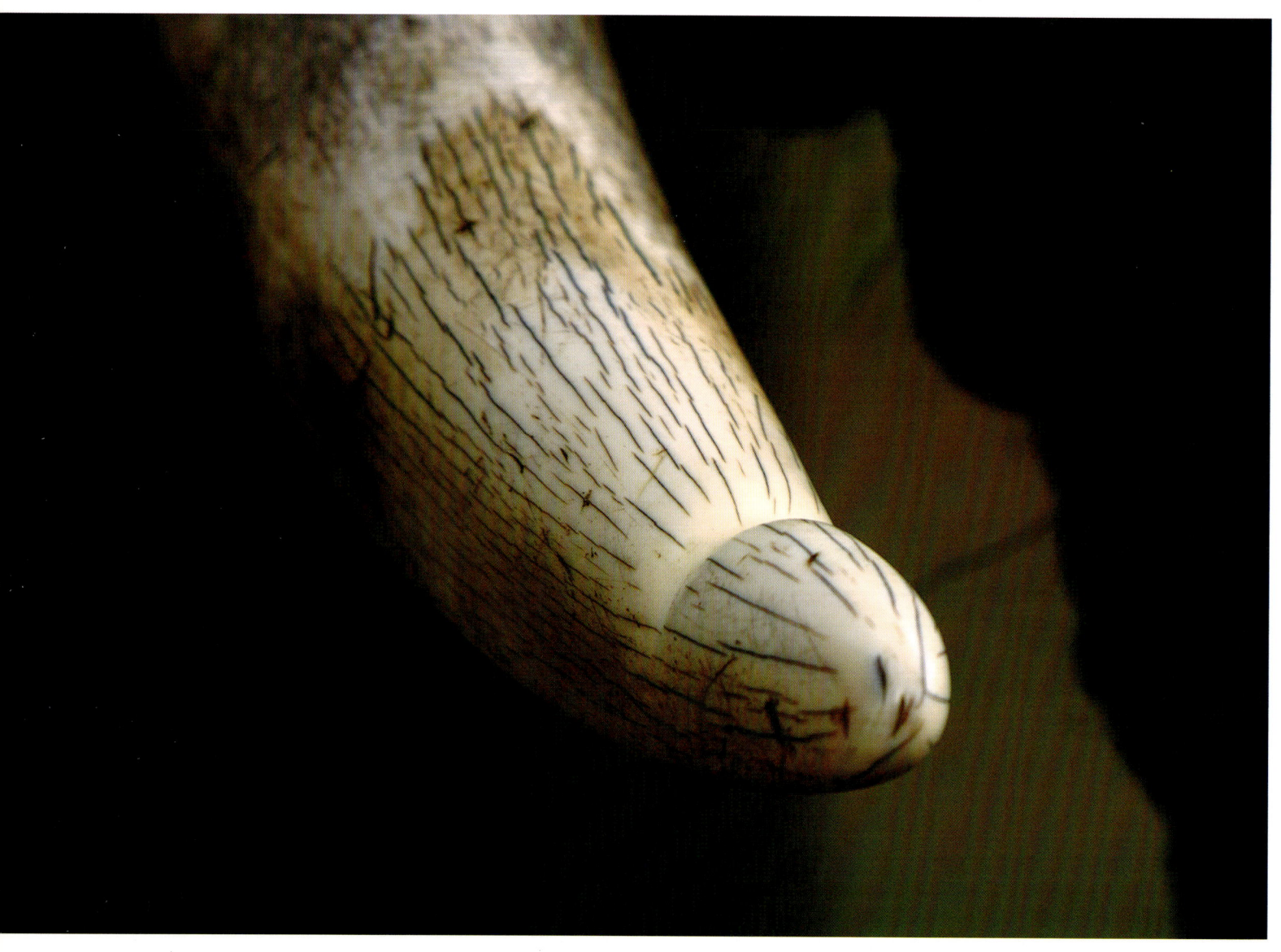

WHITE GOLD

Tusk size is genetically determined and some individuals of both sexes lack tusks. Very large and heavy tusks are an indication of advanced age. A 60-year-old bull can carry 60kg or more of ivory per tusk. One of the tusks usually shows more wear than the other, since elephants are either 'right' or 'left' tusked. Tusks, which are actually incisors, are used for defence and offence but are also important while feeding. They are used for stripping bark off trees, digging up bulbs or tubers and, together with the trunk, for breaking branches off trees.

ELEPHANT TRADEMARK

The trunk is the most unique feature of the elephant and is composed of more than 60 000 different muscles, blood vessels and a myriad of nerves. It contains no bones or cartilage. Hair and a few coarse bristles sparsely cover the thick skin, which gathers up in wrinkles as the trunk is flexed.

VERSATILE AID

The trunk is the extended union of the upper lip and nose of the African elephant. The nostrils continue from the base of the nose all the way to the tip of the trunk as two separate openings, which end in two highly sensitive and mobile finger-like extensions. The trunk is used for feeding, watering, dusting, smelling, touching and lifting. Elephants are often seen sniffing the air with their trunks, gathering information about their surroundings.

A DEXTEROUS TOOL

By simply coiling the trunk around the base of a young tree and applying force, an elephant can easily uproot it to reach the tasty roots. The front feet are sometimes used to loosen the base of shrubs.

CONSTRUCTIVE DESTRUCTION

When trees such as the maroela are laden with fruit, elephants shake them to encourage ripe fruit to drop to the ground. Sometimes individuals specialise in debarking or pushing over big trees. This can be extremely destructive if the elephant population is confined to a small area. Yet this habit can also benefit the environment, as it opens up the bush which stimulates fresh grass growth and prepares the area for utilisation by other species.

BIG EATERS

Elephants are versatile herbivores and spend up to 16 hours a day feeding. During the rainy season they prefer grasses and herbs, while they also feed on branches, leaves and tender roots, consuming five to seven percent of their body weight per day – approximately 150kg. Only 44% of what they eat will be digested. The rest emerges almost unchanged in the form of dung and provides a food source for dung beetles and other animals. Insects are, in turn, a food source for birds such as the red-billed hornbill.

IMMENSE THIRST

Visiting the waterhole is the social highlight of an elephant's day. They prefer to drink clean water and will patiently wait their turn. High-ranking individuals are the first to drink and lower-ranking elephants will yield when they approach. Water is drawn through the trunk and transferred to the mouth. The trunk can hold up to 10 litres at a time, and adult elephants may drink up to 150 litres in a single session.

FOR THE LOVE OF WATER

Elephant skin has no sweat glands and has to cool off in other ways. The large elephant body loses less heat than a smaller body does, and therefore has to

BATHING

Elephants are at home in water and can swim extremely well. They enjoy playing and frolicking, sometimes completely submerging with only the tip of the trunk out of the water.

MUDDY PLAYGROUNDS

Wallowing in muddy water is the equivalent of a spa treatment for elephants. They froth and kick up muddy water, churning it to a thick consistency, and then slap it onto their skin to act as a protective mud pack against both parasites and the hot African sun.

SKINCARE

The skin of the African elephant varies in thickness. The underside of the ears are paper thin to enable maximum cooling of the blood in the vessels directly beneath the surface. On hot days while resting or feeding, elephants will gently flap their ears to assist in cooling.

TEXTURED COAT

Elephants are pachyderms, which refers to their thick hide. In places the skin can reach a thickness of four centimetres. Over most of the body it is creased and folded, with a gnarled appearance.

POWDER POWER

Soon after bathing or wallowing, elephants cover themselves with dust. If no loose soil is in sight, they will soften soil with their front feet until enough can be scooped up with the trunk to be dusted both over and under the body. Natural elephant skin is grey to brown in colour, but tends to assume the soil colour of the wallowing or dust-bathing site. Scratching or rubbing against trees completes the skincare routine.

TIME OUT

African elephants are most active during the day, but in areas where there is much human activity, they become more nocturnal. Dust bathing is often done while resting. When sleeping, elephants usually stand upright or lean against trees, but sometimes lie down on their sides for short periods.

STURDY SUPPORT

The stout, column-like legs offer good support for the heavy body. The well-padded feet tread surprisingly silently. The rough soles are superficially cracked to form a mosaic pattern that distinguishes the spoor of individuals. African elephants have a basic ambling gait but can accelerate up to 40km/hour when charging.

OFFSPRING

A calf is born after a gestation period of 22 months and at birth it has a mass of approximately 120kg. During its long childhood the calf is nurtured by the whole family, which includes sisters and aunts, while it learns to function appropriately within the complex elephant society.

MOTHERS

The teats are situated between the forelegs, which allows the mother to interact directly with her calf while it suckles. When a cow is lactating, the nipples distend sideways and diagonally downwards to enable the newborn calf to reach them easily with its mouth.

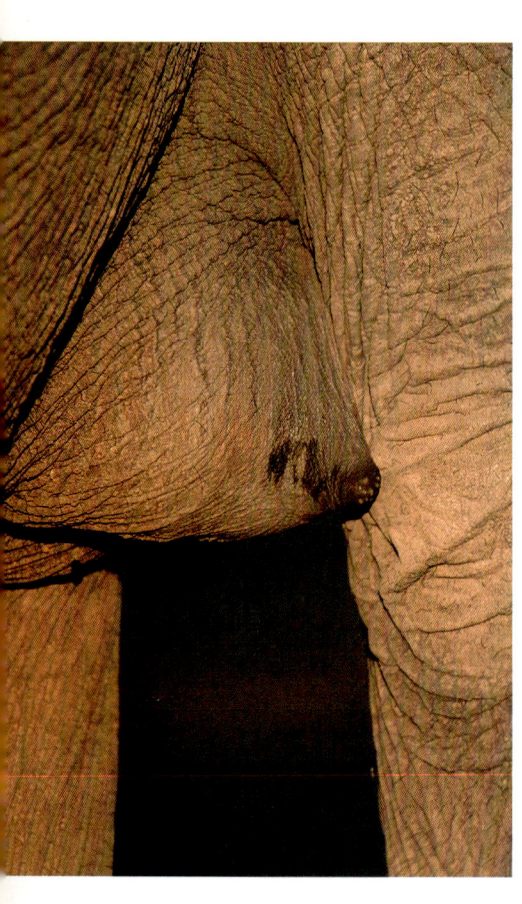

GROWING UP

The young have to learn to forage and drink with their trunks. They remain in close proximity to their mothers until they are approximately nine years old. Elephants typically reach puberty at 13 or 14 years of age. This is when young males leave the herd.

SIGNS OF EXCITEMENT

The temporal gland is situated under the skin between the eye and the ear and has a tiny opening on the temple. When the elephant gets excited, the gland secretes an oily substance, which may leak from the opening, staining the skin. Excitement can be caused by various factors such as irritation, anger, group interaction or pleasure. Bulls that are on heat are said to be in 'musth'. Bulls secreting copiously from the temporal glands, together with constant urine dribbling, are probably in musth.

A VERSATILE SPECIES

African elephants were historically found on the continent of Africa, south of the Sahara Desert all the way down to the Cape. Over the centuries, poaching and habitat destruction have taken their toll, leaving very few free-roaming elephants today. Relatively small populations now survive in national parks and private game reserves. Elephants are at home in a wide range of habitats. The most serious threat to their survival is that their needs are the same as those of people, namely food, land and water. As human populations grow, elephants are pushed into smaller and smaller sanctuaries where their own population increase soon leads to overcrowding and corresponding over-utilisation of their habitat. Ultimately, sustainable conservation management is necessary to maintain healthy populations of, and environments for, these stately creatures.

Elephants – Gentle Giants of Kapama was commissioned for the opening of Camp Jabulani at Kapama Private Game Reserve, South Africa.

Copyright © 2003 by HPH Publishing

ISBN 0-620-30488-X
First edition, first impression 2003

Published by HPH Publishing
Tel/fax: +27(0)11 704 2768
Mobile: +27(0)82 377 3849
Email: hphvdb@mweb.co.za

Photography by HPH Photography
Heinrich van den Berg
Philip & Ingrid van den Berg
Introduction by Keri Harvey
Text by Ingrid van den Berg
Edited by John Deane
Proofread by Haley Harvey
Design, typeset and reproduction by
Heinrich van den Berg, HPH Publishing
Printed and bound in Singapore by
Tien Wah Press (Pte.) Ltd

All rights reserved. No part of this publication may be reproduced or transmitted in any form or by any means without prior written permission from the publisher.